IC COOKBOOK

40+ Side dishes, Salad and Pasta recipes designed for Interstitial Cystitis Diet

TABLE OF CONTENTS

- From a Declaration of Principles which was accepted and approved equally by a Committee of the American Bar Association and a Committee of Publishers and Associations.

Introduction

IC recipes for personal enjoyment but also for family enjoyment. You will love them for sure for how easy it is to prepare them.

MINESTRONE SOUP

Serves: **6**

Prep Time: **10**   Minutes

Cook Time: **50**   Minutes

Total Time: **60**   Minutes

INGREDIENTS

- 2 onions
- 1 cup peas
- 1 can tomatoes
- 2 cups tomato sauce
- 3 carrots
- 1 cup green beans
- 2 tbs basil
- 6 cups water
- 2 cloves garlic
- Salt
- 2 tbs cheese
- 1.5 cups kidney
- 2 cups celery
- 1 bell pepper

DIRECTIONS

1. Put the onions, celery and carrots into a pot of water.

2. Add the green beans, peas, tomatoes and bell pepper when the water starts to boil, then allow to boil for 30 minutes.

3. Add the tomato sauce and basil then season with salt.

4. Allow to simmer for 10 minutes, then add the garlic and simmer for 5 more minutes.

5. Serve topped with cheese.

Serves: **4**

Prep Time: **10**   Minutes

Cook Time: **5**   Minutes

Total Time: **15**   Minutes

INGREDIENTS
- ½ tsp lemon zest
- Salt
- Pepper
- 4 eggs
- 1/3 red onion
- ¾ lb green beans
- 1 can tuna
- 1 tsp oregano
- 6 tbs olive oil
- 3 tbs lemon juice
- 1 can beans
- 1 can black olives

DIRECTIONS

1. Place the green beans, 1/3 cup water and salt to taste in a skillet.
2. Bring to a boil, covered.
3. Cook for 5 minutes.

4. Dump them onto a lined cookie sheet.

5. Mix the white beans, onion, olives and tuna.

6. Combine the oregano, lemon juice and zest, and oil in a separate bowl.

7. Pour the mixture over the tuna mixture.

8. Season and serve immediately with the boiled eggs.

Serves: **4**

Prep Time: **10** Minutes

Cook Time: **30** Minutes

Total Time: **40** Minutes

INGREDIENTS

- **1 tsp oil**
- **½ cup carrots**
- **1 zucchini**
- **1 bell pepper**
- **½ lb chicken**
- **1 onion**

DIRECTIONS

1. **Cut the chicken into strips, then cook in the oil until it gets brown.**
2. **Remove from the skillet and add the vegetables.**
3. **Cook until soft for 10 minutes, then add the chicken.**
4. **Season and serve immediately.**

SPINACH QUESADILLAS

Serves: **4**

Prep Time: **10** Minutes

Cook Time: **15** Minutes

Total Time: **25** Minutes

INGREDIENTS

- **4 cups spinach**
- **4 green onions**
- **1 tomato**
- **½ lemon juice**
- **1 tsp cumin**
- **1 tsp garlic powder**
- **Salt**
- **1 cup cheese**
- **4 tortillas**

DIRECTIONS

1. **Cook all of the ingredients except for the cheese and tortillas in a skillet.**
2. **Cook until the spinach is wilted.**
3. **Remove to a bowl and add the cheese.**
4. **Place the mixture on half of the tortilla, fold the other half and cook for 2 minutes on each side on a griddle.**

5. Serve immediately.

Serves: **4**

Prep Time: **10**   Minutes

Cook Time: **0**   Minutes

Total Time: **10**   Minutes

INGREDIENTS

- **1 can garbanzo beans**
- **1 can red beans**
- **1 tomato**
- **½ red onion**
- **½ lemon juice**
- **1 tbs olive oil**

DIRECTIONS

1. **Mix all of the ingredients together in a bowl.**
2. **Season with salt and serve immediately.**

GARLIC SALMON

Serves: **4**

Prep Time: **10** Minutes

Cook Time: **20** Minutes

Total Time: **30** Minutes

INGREDIENTS

- **2 lb salmon**
- **2 tbs water**
- **Salt**
- **2 tbs parsley**
- **4 cloves garlic**

DIRECTIONS

1. **Preheat the oven to 400F.**
2. **Mix the garlic, parsley, salt and water in a bowl.**
3. **Brush the mixture over the salmon.**
4. **Place the fish on a baking tray and cover with aluminum foil.**
5. **Cook for 20 minutes.**
6. **Serve with vegetables.**

TUNA WRAP

Serves: **4**

Prep Time: **10** Minutes

Cook Time: **0** Minutes

Total Time: **10** Minutes

INGREDIENTS

- **6 ounces tuna**
- **2 tsp yogurt**
- **½ celery stalk**
- **Handful baby spinach**
- **½ onion**
- **2 tsp lemon juice**
- **4 tortillas**

DIRECTIONS

1. Mix all of the ingredients except for the tortillas in a bowl.
2. Spread the mixture over the tortillas, then wrap them up.
3. Serve immediately.

ROASTED CHICKEN WRAP

Serves: **4**

Prep Time: **10** Minutes

Cook Time: **10** Minutes

Total Time: **20** Minutes

INGREDIENTS

- 1 cup chicken breast
- 2 tsp yogurt
- 1/3 cup celery
- 8 tomato slices
- ½ onion
- 1 tbs mustard
- 2 tbs ketchup
- 4 tortillas

DIRECTIONS

1. Cut the chicken as you desire and grill until done on each side.
2. Mix all of the ingredients except for the tortillas in a bowl.
3. Spread the mixture over the tortillas and add the chicken.
4. Serve immediately.

Serves: **4**

Prep Time: **10**   Minutes

Cook Time: **0**   Minutes

Total Time: **10**   Minutes

INGREDIENTS

- 1 cup cooked lentils
- 1 cup baby spinach
- 1 poached egg
- ¼ avocado
- ½ tomato
- 1-2 slices whole wheat bread

DIRECTIONS

1. Mix all of the ingredients together except for the bread.
2. Toast the bread.
3. Serve immediately together.

STUFFED EGGPLANT

Serves: **4**

Prep Time: **10**   Minutes

Cook Time: **50**   Minutes

Total Time: **60**   Minutes

INGREDIENTS
- 1 eggplant
- 2 onions
- 1 red pepper
- ½ cup tomato juice
- ¼ cup cheese

DIRECTIONS

1. Preheat the oven to 350F.
2. Cut the eggplant in half and cook for 30 minutes.
3. Cook the diced onion in 2 tbs of water until brown.
4. Add the pepper and add it to the onion, cooking for another 5 minutes.
5. Add the tomato juice and allow to cook for another 5 minutes.
6. Scoop out the eggplant.
7. Mix the eggplant with the onion mixture, then add it back into the eggplant shell.
8. Grate the cheese on top and bake for another 10 minutes.
9. Serve hot.

Serves: 2

Prep Time: 5   Minutes

Cook Time: 20   Minutes

Total Time: 25   Minutes

INGREDIENTS

- **1 tbs olive oil**
- **¼ tsp thyme**
- **1 cup arugula**
- **½ lemon juice**
- **1 head broccoli**
- **1 clove garlic**
- **2 cups water**
- **¼ tsp salt**
- **¼ tsp black pepper**
- **½ yellow onion**

DIRECTIONS

1. Heat the oil in a saucepan.
2. Cook the onion until soft, then add the garlic and cook for another minute.
3. Add the broccoli and cook for 5 minutes.
4. Add the water, thyme, salt, and pepper.

5. Bring to boil, then lower the heat and cook for 10 minutes.

6. Transfer to a blender, blend, then add the arugula and blend until smooth.

7. Add the lemon juice and serve immediately.

Serves: **4**

Prep Time: **20** Minutes

Cook Time: **25** Minutes

Total Time: **45** Minutes

INGREDIENTS

- ½ onion
- 1 cup mushrooms
- ½ yellow bell pepper
- 1 cup spinach
- 1 can tomatoes
- 1 tbs tomato paste
- 4 red bell peppers
- 1 lb ground turkey
- 2 tbs olive oil
- 1 zucchini
- ½ green bell pepper
- 1 tsp Italian seasoning
- ½ tsp garlic powder
- Salt
- Pepper

DIRECTIONS

1. Bring a pot of water to a boil.
2. Cut the tops off the peppers, and remove the seeds.
3. Cook in water for 5 minutes.
4. Preheat the oven to 350F.
5. Cook the turkey until brown.
6. Heat the oil and cook the onion, mushrooms, zucchini, green and yellow pepper, and spinach until soft.
7. Add the turkey and the rest of the ingredients.
8. Stuff the peppers with the mixture.
9. Bake for 15 minutes.
10. Serve hot.

POTATO SALAD

Serves: **6**

Prep Time: **5** Minutes

Cook Time: **10** Minutes

Total Time: **15** Minutes

INGREDIENTS

- **1 red onion**
- **2 tsp cumin seeds**
- **1 cloves garlic**
- **½ cup olive oil**
- **4 potatoes**
- **½ cup lemon juice**
- **2 tbs fresh parsley**
- **1 ½ tsp salt**
- **2 tsp turmeric powder**

DIRECTIONS

1. **Steam the potatoes for 10 minutes, until tender.**
2. **Mix the lemon juice, turmeric, cumin seeds, and salt.**
3. **Place the potatoes in a bowl and pour the mixture over.**
4. **Add the onion and garlic and stir to coat.**
5. **Refrigerate until the potatoes are cold.**

6. Add olive oil and herbs and stir.

Serves: *4*
Prep Time: *20*   Minutes

Cook Time: *10*   Minutes

Total Time: *30*   Minutes

INGREDIENTS

- 1 cucumber
- 1 cup red cabbage
- 1 ½ lbs ground pork
- 6 radishes
- 4 tsp sugar
- 2 tbs olive oil
- ¼ cup white wine vinegar
- 2 tbs soy sauce
- 2 tsp garlic powder
- 2 tbs sesame oil
- 4 scallions
- 2 tsp Sriracha
- 12 tortillas
- 2 tsp cilantro
- ½ cup sour cream
- Salt
- Pepper

DIRECTIONS

1. Place the cucumbers, radishes, vinegar, 2 tsp sugar, salt, and pepper in a bowl.

2. Cook the scallions and cabbage in the oil until soft.

3. Add the pork, garlic powder, and 2 tsp sugar and cook for another 5 minutes.

4. Add the sesame oil, Sriracha, soy sauce and combine.

5. Season with salt and pepper.

6. Heat the tortillas in the microwave for a few seconds.

7. Spread sour cream on the tortilla, add the mixture, sprinkle cilantro over and add the cucumber and radishes.

8. Serve immediately.

Serves: **4**

Prep Time: **10**   Minutes

Cook Time: **25**   Minutes

Total Time: **40**   Minutes

INGREDIENTS

- 1 lb. ground lamb
- 1 egg
- 1 cloves garlic
- 1 handful parsley
- 1 tablespoon dried oregano
- 1 tsp dried rosemary
- ½ cup fetta cheese
- ¼ tsp salt

DIRECTIONS

1. Preheat the oven to 325 F
2. In a bowl mix all ingredients
3. Form into meat balls
4. Bake for 20-25 minutes, remove and serve

BAKED CHILLI CHICKEN

Serves: **4**

Prep Time: **10**   Minutes

Cook Time: **30**   Minutes

Total Time: **40**   Minutes

INGREDIENTS

- 2 lb. chicken drumsticks
- 3 tablespoons olive oil
- 2 cloves garlic
- 2 tablespoons lime juice
- 3 tsp lime zest
- 1 tsp chilli flakes
- salt

DIRECTIONS

1. In a bowl place all ingredients except chicken drumsticks
2. Refrigerate and then add the drumsticks for 1-2 hours
3. Preheat oven to 350 F
4. Arrange the chicken drumsticks on a greased oven tray and bake for 40-45 minutes
5. Remove and serve

Serves: *2*
Prep Time: *10*   Minutes

Cook Time: *15*   Minutes

Total Time: *25*   Minutes

INGREDIENTS

- 1 head broccoli
- 1 handful cashews
- 1 tablespoons macadamia nut oil
- 2 tablespoons coconut aminos
- 1 tablespoon fish sauce
- 2 cloves garlic
- ¼ red pepper
- 1 tablespoon lime juice
- 6 oz. shrimp
- 1 tablespoon sesame seeds
- salt

DIRECTIONS

1. In a frying pan heat oil over medium heat
2. Add garlic, sesame seeds, red pepper and cashews
3. Add shrimp and fry for 3-4 minutes

4. Remove and serve

SPINACH FRITATTA

Serves: **2**

Prep Time: **10** Minutes

Cook Time: **20** Minutes

Total Time: **30** Minutes

INGREDIENTS

- ½ lb. spinach
- 1 tablespoon olive oil
- ½ red onion
- 2 eggs
- ¼ tsp salt
- 2 oz. cheddar cheese
- 1 garlic clove
- ¼ tsp dill

DIRECTIONS

1. In a bowl whisk eggs with salt and cheese
2. In a frying pan heat olive oil and pour egg mixture
3. Add remaining ingredients and mix well
4. Serve when ready

TURNIP FRITATTA

Serves: *2*

Prep Time: *10*   Minutes

Cook Time: *20*   Minutes

Total Time: *30*   Minutes

INGREDIENTS

- ½ lb. spinach
- ¼ cup turnip
- ½ red onion
- 2 eggs
- ¼ tsp salt
- 2 oz. cheddar cheese
- 1 garlic clove
- ¼ tsp dill

DIRECTIONS

1. In a bowl whisk eggs with salt and cheese
2. In a frying pan heat olive oil and pour egg mixture
3. Add remaining ingredients and mix well
4. Serve when ready

Serves: **2**

Prep Time: **10** Minutes

Cook Time: **20** Minutes

Total Time: **30** Minutes

INGREDIENTS

- 1 cup squash
- 1 tablespoon olive oil
- ½ red onion
- 2 eggs
- ¼ tsp salt
- 2 oz. cheddar cheese
- 1 garlic clove
- ¼ tsp dill

DIRECTIONS

1. In a bowl whisk eggs with salt and cheese
2. In a frying pan heat olive oil and pour egg mixture
3. Add remaining ingredients and mix well
4. Serve when ready

HAM FRITATTA

Serves: *2*

Prep Time: *10*   Minutes

Cook Time: *20*   Minutes

Total Time: *30*   Minutes

INGREDIENTS

- 8-10 slices ham
- 1 tablespoon olive oil
- ½ red onion
- 2 eggs
- ¼ tsp salt
- 2 oz. parmesan cheese
- 1 garlic clove
- ¼ tsp dill

DIRECTIONS

1. In a bowl whisk eggs with salt and parmesan cheese
2. In a frying pan heat olive oil and pour egg mixture
3. Add remaining ingredients and mix well
4. When prosciutto and eggs are cooked remove from heat and serve

Serves: **2**

Prep Time: **10** Minutes

Cook Time: **20** Minutes

Total Time: **30** Minutes

INGREDIENTS

- 1 tablespoon olive oil
- ½ red onion
- 2 eggs
- ¼ tsp salt
- 2 oz. cheddar cheese
- 1 garlic clove
- ¼ tsp dill

DIRECTIONS

1. In a bowl whisk eggs with salt and cheese
2. In a frying pan heat olive oil and pour egg mixture
3. Add remaining ingredients and mix well
4. Serve when ready

FRIED CHICKEN WITH ALMONDS

Serves: 2

Prep Time: *10*   Minutes

Cook Time: 25   Minutes

Total Time: 35   Minutes

INGREDIENTS

- 1 cup bread crumbs
- ¼ cup parmesan cheese
- ¼ cup almonds
- 1 tsp salt
- 1 tablespoon parley leaves
- 1 clove garlic
- ½ cup olive oil
- 2 lb. chicken breast

DIRECTIONS

1. In a bowl combine parsley, almonds, garlic, parmesan, bread crumbs, salt and mix well
2. In a bowl add olive oil and dip chicken breast into olive oil
3. Place chicken into the breadcrumb mixture and toss to coat
4. Bake chicken at 375 F for 20-25 minutes
5. When ready remove chicken from the oven and serve

FILET MIGNON WITH TOMATO SAUCE

Serves: **4**

Prep Time: **10**   Minutes

Cook Time: **30**   Minutes

Total Time: **40**   Minutes

INGREDIENTS

- 1 tsp soy sauce
- 1 tsp mustard
- 1 tsp parsley leaves
- 1 clove garlic
- 2-3 tomatoes
- 2 tsp olive oil
- 4-5 beef tenderloin steaks
- ½ tsp salt

DIRECTIONS

1. In a bowl combine parsley, garlic, soy sauce, mustard and mix well
2. Stir in tomatoes slices and toss to coat
3. In a skillet heat olive oil and place the steak
4. Cook until golden brown for 3-4 minutes
5. Transfer skillet to the oven and bake at 375 F for 8-10 minutes
6. When ready remove and serve with tomato sauce

ZUCCHINI NOODLES

Serves: *1*
Prep Time: 5   Minutes

Cook Time: *15*   Minutes

Total Time: *20*   Minutes

INGREDIENTS

- 2 zucchinis
- 1 tablespoon olive oil
- 1 garlic clove
- ½ cup parmesan cheese
- 1 tsp salt

DIRECTIONS

1. Spiralize zucchini and set aside
2. In a skillet melt butter, add garlic and zucchini noodles
3. Toss to coat and cook for 5-6 minutes
4. When ready remove from the skillet and serve with parmesan cheese on top

GREEN BEANS WITH TOMATOES

Serves: **4**

Prep Time: **10** Minutes

Cook Time: **15** Minutes

Total Time: **25** Minutes

INGREDIENTS

- 1 cup water
- 1 lb. green beans
- 2 tomatoes
- 1 tsp olive oil
- 1 tsp Italian dressing
- salt

DIRECTIONS

1. In a pot bring water to a boil
2. Add green beans, tomatoes and boil for 10-12 minutes
3. Remove green beans and tomatoes to a bowl
4. Chop tomatoes, add Italian dressing, olive oil and serve

ROASTED CAULIFLOWER RICE

Serves: **2**

Prep Time: **10**   Minutes

Cook Time: **25**   Minutes

Total Time: **35**   Minutes

INGREDIENTS

- 3-4 cups frozen cauliflower rice
- 1 tablespoon olive oil
- 2 garlic cloves
- ½ cup parmesan cheese

DIRECTIONS

1. Place the cauliflower rice on a sheet pan
2. Sprinkle garlic and olive oil over the cauliflower rice and toss well
3. Spread cauliflower rice in a single layer in the pan
4. Roast cauliflower rice at 375 F for 20-25 minutes
5. When ready remove from the oven and serve with parmesan cheese on top

ROASTED SQUASH

Serves:	**3-4**	
Prep Time:	**10**	Minutes
Cook Time:	**20**	Minutes
Total Time:	**30**	Minutes

INGREDIENTS

- 2 delicata squashes
- 2 tablespoons olive oil
- 1 tsp curry powder
- 1 tsp salt

DIRECTIONS

1. Preheat the oven to 400 F
2. Cut everything in half lengthwise
3. Toss everything with olive oil and place onto a prepared baking sheet
4. Roast for 18-20 minutes at 400 F or until golden brown
5. When ready remove from the oven and serve

Serves: 2

Prep Time: *10*   Minutes

Cook Time: *20*   Minutes

Total Time: *30*   Minutes

INGREDIENTS

- 1 lb. brussels sprouts
- 1 tablespoon olive oil
- 1 tablespoon parmesan cheese
- 1 tsp garlic powder
- 1 tsp seasoning

DIRECTIONS

1. Preheat the oven to 425 F
2. In a bowl toss everything with olive oil and seasoning
3. Spread everything onto a prepared baking sheet
4. Bake for 8-10 minutes or until crisp
5. When ready remove from the oven and serve

SQUASH CHIPS

Serves: **2**

Prep Time: **10**   Minutes

Cook Time: **20**   Minutes

Total Time: **30**   Minutes

INGREDIENTS

- 1 lb. squash
- 1 tablespoon olive oil
- 1 tsp garlic powder
- 1 tsp seasoning

DIRECTIONS

1. Preheat the oven to 425 F
2. In a bowl toss everything with olive oil and seasoning
3. Spread everything onto a prepared baking sheet
4. Bake for 8-10 minutes or until crisp
5. When ready remove from the oven and serve

Serves: 2

Prep Time: *10* Minutes

Cook Time: *20* Minutes

Total Time: *30* Minutes

INGREDIENTS

- 1 lb. zucchini
- 1 tablespoon olive oil
- 1 tablespoon parmesan cheese
- 1 tsp garlic powder
- 1 tsp seasoning

DIRECTIONS

1. Preheat the oven to 425 F
2. In a bowl toss everything with olive oil and seasoning
3. Spread everything onto a prepared baking sheet
4. Bake for 8-10 minutes or until crisp
5. When ready remove from the oven and serve

Serves: *2*
Prep Time: *10*   Minutes

Cook Time: *20*   Minutes

Total Time: *30*   Minutes

INGREDIENTS

- 1 lb. carrot
- 1 tablespoon olive oil
- 1 tablespoon parmesan cheese
- 1 tsp garlic powder
- 1 tsp seasoning

DIRECTIONS

1. Preheat the oven to 425 F
2. In a bowl toss everything with olive oil and seasoning
3. Spread everything onto a prepared baking sheet
4. Bake for 8-10 minutes or until crisp
5. When ready remove from the oven and serve

PASTA

SIMPLE SPAGHETTI

Serves: **2**

Prep Time: **5**   Minutes

Cook Time: **15**   Minutes

Total Time: **20**   Minutes

INGREDIENTS

- 10 oz. spaghetti
- 2 eggs
- ½ cup parmesan cheese
- 1 tsp black pepper
- Olive oil
- 1 tsp parsley
- 2 cloves garlic

DIRECTIONS

1. In a pot boil spaghetti (or any other type of pasta), drain and set aside
2. In a bowl whish eggs with parmesan cheese
3. In a skillet heat olive oil, add garlic and cook for 1-2 minutes
4. Pour egg mixture and mix well
5. Add pasta and stir well

6. When ready garnish with parsley and serve

Serves: 2

Prep Time: 5   Minutes

Cook Time: 15   Minutes

Total Time: 20   Minutes

INGREDIENTS

- ¼ cup olive oil
- 1 jar artichokes
- 2 cloves garlic
- 1 tablespoon thyme leaves
- 1 lb. pasta
- 2 tablespoons butter
- 1. Cup basil
- ½ cup parmesan cheese

DIRECTIONS

1. In a pot boil spaghetti (or any other type of pasta), drain and set aside
2. Place all the ingredients for the sauce in a pot and bring to a simmer
3. Add pasta and mix well
4. When ready garnish with parmesan cheese and serve

CHICKEN PASTA

Serves: **2**

Prep Time: **5**   Minutes

Cook Time: **15**   Minutes

Total Time: **20**   Minutes

INGREDIENTS

- 1 lb. cooked chicken breast
- 8 oz. pasta
- 2 tablespoons butter
- 1 tablespoon garlic
- 1 tablespoon flour
- ½ cup milk
- ½ cup heavy cream
- 1 jar red bell peppers
- 2 tablespoons basil

DIRECTIONS

1. In a pot boil spaghetti (or any other type of pasta), drain and set aside
2. Place all the ingredients for the sauce in a pot and bring to a simmer
3. Add pasta and mix well
4. When ready garnish with parmesan cheese and serve

SALAD RECIPES

MEDITERRANEAN TUNA SALAD

Serves: **4**

Prep Time: **10**   Minutes

Cook Time: **30**   Minutes

Total Time: **40**   Minutes

INGREDIENTS

- 2 cans tuna
- 2 celery stalks
- 1 cucumber
- 4 radishes
- 2 onions
- 1 red onion
- ¼ Kalamata olives
- 1 bunch parsley
- 10 mint leaves
- 1 tomato
- 1 serving mustard vinaigrette

DIRECTIONS

1. In a bowl combine all ingredients together
2. Add salad dressing and serve

MEXICAN TUNA SALAD

Serves: **2**

Prep Time: **5** Minutes

Cook Time: **5** Minutes

Total Time: **10** Minutes

INGREDIENTS

- 2 cans tuna
- 1 red bell pepper
- 1 can black beans
- 1 can black olives
- 1 can yellow corn
- 2 tomatoes
- 2 avocados

DRESSING

- ½ cup Greek yogurt
- ¼ cup mayonnaise
- 1 tsp garlic powder
- ¼ tsp cumin

DIRECTIONS

1. In a bowl combine all ingredients together
2. In another bowl combine all ingredients for the dressing

3. Add dressing, mix well and serve

PRAWN NOODLE SALAD

Serves: **4**

Prep Time: **10** Minutes

Cook Time: **10** Minutes

Total Time: **20** Minutes

INGREDIENTS

- ¼ lbs. noodle
- ¼ lbs. baby spinach
- 3 oz. cooked prawn
- ¼ lbs. snap pea
- 1 carrot

DRESSING

- 1 red chili
- 1 tsp fish sauce
- 1 tablespoon mint
- 2 tablespoons rice vinegar
- 1 tsp sugar

DIRECTIONS

1. In a bowl add all dressing ingredients and mix well
2. In another bowl add salad ingredients and mix well, pour dressing over salad and serve

ARUGULA AND SWEET POTATO SALAD

Serves: 2

Prep Time: **10** Minutes

Cook Time: **15** Minutes

Total Time: **25** Minutes

INGREDIENTS

- 1 lb. sweet potatoes
- 1 cup walnuts
- 1 tablespoon olive oil
- 1 cup water
- 1 tablespoon soy sauce
- 3 cups arugula

DIRECTIONS

1. Bake potatoes at 400 F until tender, remove and set aside
2. In a bowl drizzle, walnuts with olive oil and microwave for 2-3 minutes or until toasted
3. In a bowl combine all salad ingredients and mix well
4. Pour over soy sauce and serve

Serves: **4**

Prep Time: **10** Minutes

Cook Time: **30** Minutes

Total Time: **40** Minutes

INGREDIENTS

- 2 mangoes
- Juice of 1 lemon
- ¼ onion
- 1 tablespoon cilantro laves

DIRECTIONS

1. In a bowl combine all salad ingredients and mix well
2. Add salad dressing and serve when ready

COUSCOUS SALAD

Serves: **4**

Prep Time: **10** Minutes

Cook Time: **30** Minutes

Total Time: **40** Minutes

INGREDIENTS

- 1 cup couscous
- 1 cup zucchini
- 1 red bell pepper
- ¼ cup red onion
- ¼ tsp cumin
- ¼ tsp black pepper
- ¼ cup salad dressing
- ¼ tsp parsley

DIRECTIONS

1. In a bowl combine all salad ingredients and mix well
2. Add salad dressing and serve when ready

Serves: **4**

Prep Time: **10** Minutes

Cook Time: **30** Minutes

Total Time: **40** Minutes

INGREDIENTS

- 1 oz. red potatoes
- 1 package green beans
- 2 eggs
- ½ cup tomatoes
- 2 tablespoons wine vinegar
- ¼ tsp salt
- ½ tsp pepper
- ½ tsp thyme
- ¼ cup olive oil
- 6 oz. tuna
- ¼ cup Kalamata olives

DIRECTIONS

1. In a bowl combine all ingredients together
2. Add salad dressing and serve

Serves: **2**

Prep Time: **10**   Minutes

Cook Time: **30**   Minutes

Total Time: **40**   Minutes

INGREDIENTS

- ¼ cup lemon juice
- ¼ cup rice wine vinegar
- 1 tsp sugar
- 1 cucumber
- ¼ cup mint
- 10 oz. cooked crab
- 2 cups mixed salad greens
- 2 lime wedges

DIRECTIONS

1. In a bowl combine all salad ingredients and mix well
2. Add salad dressing and serve when ready

THANK YOU FOR READING THIS BOOK!